Greek Mythology for Kids: From the Gods to the Titans

Speedy Publishing LLC
40 E. Main St. #1156
Newark, DE 19711
www.speedypublishing.com

The Olympians are a group of 12 gods who ruled after the overthow of the Titans.

Zeus was the king of the Greek gods who lived on Mount Olympus. His most famous power is the ability to throw lightning bolts.

Poseidon rules over the ocean and all bodies of water. Poseidon's weapon is the trident, and he uses it to shatter any object and shake the earth.

Hades ruled the Underworld, the world of the dead. Hades had a giant three-headed dog named Cerberus. Cerberus guarded the entrance to the Underworld.

Athena was most famous for being the patron god of the city of Athens. Athena was also a goddess of wisdom. Athena was often depicted as a warrior goddess armed with a spear, a shield, and a helmet.

Hera was the queen of the gods and the protector of women. She was the patron goddess of the city of Argos.

Ares is the son of Zeus and Hera. He is the Greek god of war. He was known for being violent and cruel, but also cowardly.

Apollo is the
Greek god of
music, poetry,
light, prophecy,
and medicine.
Apollo was
also known as
great healer.

Aphrodite is the Greek goddess of love and beauty. She is famous for being the most beautiful of the goddesses.

Hermes was
the messenger
god. He wore a
winged hat and
winged sandals,
and he carried
a magic wand.
Hermes is a god
of transitions
and boundaries.

Artemis is goddess of the moon and of the hunt. She is the twin sister of the god Apollo. She often is shown accompanied by forest creatures such as deer and bears.

Oceanus is believed to be the divine personification of the sea, an enormous river encircling the world. Oceanus was the eldest of the Titans.

Prometheus is
known in Greek
mythology as
the creator
of mankind.
He also gave
mankind the
gift of fire from
Mount Olympus.

Atlas led the Titanes in a rebellion against Zeus and was condemned to bear the heavens upon his shoulders.

Themis is an ancient
Greek Titaness. She is the
personification of divine
order, law, natural law and
custom. She was mother to
the Fates and the Hours.